# MAKE THEM BELIEVERS

## BUSINESS BRANDING & STRATEGY WORKBOOK

**NATASHA T. BROWN**     **CARESSA JENNINGS**

---

**IDEAL FOR**
Business Owners who Need a Solid Brand Foundation
Authors who want to Write and Publish Bestselling Books
Marketplace Ministers who Plan to Impact the World
Coaches & Brands that Want to Attract High Paying Clients

Copyright© 2017 Natasha T. Brown and Caressa Jennings

All rights reserved. No portion of this book may be reproduced in any form without the written permission of the authors, except for brief excerpts for review purposes.

Contact Information for Bulk Orders and Course Registration:

www.makethembelievers.co
info@makethembelievers.co

*Visit MakeThemBelievers.co to register for the companion course - Make Them Believers Virtual Retreat or search for individual courses that correspond with each chapter.*

Caressa J.  www.caressaj.com
Natasha T. Brown www.natashatbrown.com

Scripture quotations are from the ESV® Bible (The Holy Bible, English Standard Version®), copyright © 2001 by Crossway, a publishing ministry of Good News Publishers. Used by permission. All rights reserved.

Scripture taken from the New King James Version®. Copyright © 1982 by Thomas Nelson. Used by permission. All rights reserved.

Scripture taken from the Amplified Bible, Copyright © 1954, 1958, 1962, 1964, 1965, 1987 by The Lockman Foundation. Used by permission.

Published by Brown & Duncan Brand | BandDBrand.com
ISBN: 978-0-9992023-9-5

Printed in the United States of America

# DEDICATION

We dedicate this book to the amazing women who are constantly looking straight ahead despite the many obstacles you have faced while fulfilling your God-given purpose. Everything you ask for will be given to you (John 14:13). You are the answer to several prayers. Keep going!

## ACKNOWLEDGEMENTS

We acknowledge our spiritual parents and mentors. If it were not for you, we would have talked ourselves out of the purposes that God has predestined for us. To Drs. Mike and DeeDee Freeman of Spirit of Faith Christian Center in Maryland and Bishop Stephanie Stratford of Ekklesia International in Brentwood, Maryland, we thank you for your consistent teachings on faith and your dedication to living the Word. The examples you have set in ministry and the marketplace are remarkable and have inspired us more than you know. Thank you!

We would also like to acknowledge the amazing women who enrolled in our first Make Them Believers Academy Virtual Retreat in October of 2017. You completely blew our minds with the transformation you experienced in a weekend. Your commitment and dedication to your books, brands, missions, and ministries are going to have a deep impact for generations to come. We can't wait to see you soar!

# CONTENTS

Introduction: Ministry in the Marketplace ............................................................... 7

Chapter 1: Mindset to Monetize .................................................................................. 17

Chapter 2: Brand Foundation ...................................................................................... 25

Chapter 3: The Author's Masterclass ........................................................................ 41

Chapter 4: Cut through the Noise to be Heard ....................................................... 57

Chapter 5: Pitch Like a Pro .......................................................................................... 61

Chapter 6: D.I.Y. OR PAY-TO-PLAY? ........................................................................... 65

Topical Scripture Glossary for Believers in Business ............................................ 73

About the Authors .......................................................................................................... 85

*"For we are his workmanship, created in Christ Jesus for good works, which God prepared beforehand, that we should walk in them."*
Ephesians 2:10

# INTRODUCTION
# MINISTRY IN THE MARKETPLACE

Are you ready to embark on a journey of a lifetime? Okay, let's get started. We are excited that you are joining us on this at-home retreat. If you find *Make Them Believers* helpful, please let others know how they can get a copy.

Now, imagine there is a bald eagle who was adopted by a family of ducks. As a youngster, the Eagle, (let's call her Ellen) watched as the baby ducks in her family grew feathers and blossomed into full-grown mallards. They tended to love the water and were not into hanging in the sky or participating in any of the activities that Ellen wanted to explore. Over time, Ellen grew so accustomed to the lifestyle of ducks that she never tapped into the innate abilities that she inherited from her own species. However, Ellen realized that she looked and sounded different than the others around her. Even her feathers felt much different than the ducks whom she grew up with. Ellen began to feel rejected and simply out of place. She knew that she was unique and different from the others in her family, but she couldn't pinpoint why.

Not long after Ellen the Eagle grew old enough to venture off on her own, she began to explore the area surrounding the island where her home was located. One day, as Ellen was out searching for food for her family, she saw a bird from a distance that seemed unknown, yet familiar to her. Grabbing her attention, Ellen watched as this other magnificent creature, Bruce the eagle, flew high and then came back down low to scoop fish. Once Bruce landed, Ellen went over to him and said, "Wow, that was something. I wish that I could fly as high as you."

"Oh but you can, dear. You are an eagle. You can fly up to ten thousand feet into the air, so high that the creatures down here wouldn't see you."

"A what?" she asked him.

"An eagle. You are an eagle!" Bruce thought Ellen was strange at this point, but nevertheless he was eager to get her on the right track. "What's your name? Are you telling me that you've never flown that high before?" Bruce asked her.

Ellen told Bruce that she had always remained close to the grown, no more than about two to four hundred feet from land and she was never taught to fly so high, because she was just an abnormal mallard. Over the next hour, Bruce shared some things with Ellen. He let her know how special she was. For the first time, Ellen came to the realization that she was an eagle and not a duck, and suddenly her entire life made sense to her. As an eagle, Bruce shared, Ellen had the gift of not only flying above the other birds in the land, but she also had the natural gift of vision. In fact, if she flew high enough, Ellen learned that she could see up to two to five miles in the distance. This was significant, because although the ducks around her also had great sight, they were too low to the ground to truly activate vision. Ellen was so excited to learn about her gifts of flight and vision, and once she gathered food for her family back home, Ellen let them know that she would be leaving to discover her true purpose. Ellen had come face-to-face with her identity, and she finally found her place in the world! There was nothing like this feeling, and there was no way that she could go back to the life she knew after getting a glimpse of what she could do.

Being a believer who has discovered the true reason why God created you is similar to being like Ellen the eagle. Chances are, if you are just awakening to purpose or if you've been blessed with the burden of a new idea from God, you feel a lot like Ellen… out of place until you can pinpoint exactly how to bridge the gap between your purpose and the present path. Perhaps you've finally realized your true identity and are ready to tap into God's true purpose for your life, but like Ellen, you need someone like Bruce who will coach you to your next level. If this sounds like you, you are in the right place!

The mission of **Make Them Believers Academy** (and this at-home retreat and workbook) is to equip believers to excel in business and life by offering intimate learning experiences that build marketplace ministers, such as yourself, both spiritually and professionally. **We want to help you *Make Them Believers* of you, the purpose God has created you for, and as a result, the Lord Jesus Christ.** We believe that God has appointed believers to arise and represent the kingdom of God in the marketplace and that we all have a unique role in turning hearts back to God.

This workbook will be one that you can revisit to build your faith, expand your thinking, and assist you in <u>implementing the passions that God has placed within you, including launching your business, building your brand, and writing and publishing your bestselling books.</u>

**You are Embarking on a Personal, Spiritual, Business Retreat**
Each chapter, including this one, is designed to serve as one personal retreat or class experience for you. In other words, you want to take time on this, working through the activities, meditating on what we've written, and carefully considering the principles discussed. If you attempt to read this like a regular book, you will have missed the point of this resource. We urge you to work through it patiently.

**God the CEO**

Before we get into the business principles and strategies that will help you *Make Them Believers,* let's first explore the role of God in business. As a believer, God will give you divine strategies to help you reach those who He wants to experience his heart. It's important that no matter what you deal with through this entrepreneurial journey that you never forget that important truth. You will be tempted to operate in your own strength, follow trends, take worldly advice, and copy others who appear to be successful. At all costs, avoid these tactics if you are not receiving confirmation in your spirit from the Holy Spirit. Remember the words of Proverbs 16:9, *"In their hearts humans plan their course, but the LORD establishes their steps."* God's main goal is to establish a big family through us His children, and He uses each of us to help others to experience the gospel and His love in a variety of ways. We are called to do this through our creative and business endeavors.

If He is not now, God must become the CEO of your business, starting today. This is easy to say and often less easier to do. This means that instead of operating in our own emotions, knowledge, and feelings, with God as the CEO, we must constantly ask the question, *What Would Jesus Do?*

**STOP HERE AND BRAINSTORM ON STEPS TO MAKE GOD YOUR CEO.**

___

**Prayer**

As the CEO of your business, God will desire to meet with you, just like any other CEO would his employees. These meetings will be unlike any you've ever had, because they will become times that you will literally tap into the heart and mind of God for the business/purpose He has assigned to you. Psalm 112:1-3 tells us that, *"Unless the Lord builds the house, those who build it labor in vain. Unless the Lord watches over the city, the watchman stays awake in vain."* This is a critical point to highlight, because unless God becomes the CEO of your business, everything you build will be in vain.

Meetings with God and hearing from Him will be the deciding factor to determine whether you be successful or if instead you will build a business "in vain." Another important point to add is that success does not equate to money. It can include monetary wealth, but true success is doing what God has purposed for your life.

In order to hear God, of course, we must be in His word, as the Word of God is the main way that He speaks to us. Another way is through prayer. The Word tells us to pray without ceasing, and this is the rule of thumb for entrepreneurship. Literally pray about EVERYTHING.

Both of us, (Caressa and Natasha) have dealt with anxiety. For me, (Natasha) some of the main times when the enemy has sent these anxious feelings my way has been immediately before my strategy and planning meetings with clients. As someone who doesn't like to fail, I would often get anxiety before speaking with clients, because the enemy would plant thoughts of failure in my head. Satan is the author of lies, and the truth is that even if something were to go wrong, there is nothing that God cannot fix. Luke 1:37 tells us that *with God, nothing will be impossible*. I have learned to overcome this anxiety through prayer.

At one point, I remember dealing with a really difficult client. It seemed liked no matter what I did, or how many resources that I provided to make sure this person's vision came to life, the client wasn't happy. I was extremely anxious and often very upset when I dealt with the client. I didn't even want to proceed because of a fear that I had failed, when in reality, this person was simply unreasonable, and was being influenced by anxious thoughts that the enemy had planted within their own mind. In addition, this person's lack of planning and unreasonable timeline was projected on me. Instead of praying prior to agreeing to help with the project, I said "yes," without establishing boundaries. I didn't realize this until I reviewed the situation in hindsight. However, this situation made me realize the importance of praying through every step of my interactions with my clients and especially before every deal I agreed to.

Once I became more connected with the Word, I began to realize the true meaning of praying without ceasing. Today, not only do I pray before client meetings and pray for the overall success of my businesses, but I also pray for my clients' businesses, for their success, their peace, that they will have a global impact, and that our work together will help catapult them to their next place of glory. I pray for protection in business, provision, and for God to give me strategies to teach and share. A long time ago, the Lord told me that I was a *Communicator for Christ.* Therefore, I realize that the nature, message, and timing of my communication is critical for the kingdom. I pray before I ghostwrite and edit books, and prior to pressing play on live broadcasts or stepping up to a podium to speak or teach.

Prayer will empower you to move in a divine confidence, knowing that as you have prayed without ceasing, the Lord has downloaded ideas, direction, and wisdom into your spirit daily.

In the back of this book, you will find a **Scripture Glossary for Entrepreneurs.** If you would like assistance or are unsure of how to pray for and in your business, we encourage you to write prayers that include these scriptures. ***Praying the Word of God is the best way to begin an open line of communication with Him***. As you pray for your business, remember to take time to get in a quiet place with God so that you can hear as He speaks back to you--this "quiet time" can be a few minutes, an entire day, or even weeks at a time. During various times of our entrepreneurial journeys, the Lord has instructed both of us to take time away from social media and other indulgences, remove the clutter of the world, and just listen. Don't limit God and be sure that you are always in a posture to hear from Him.

## Planning

As prayer becomes the foundation of your business, one aspect that you will become aware of are His plans for you and your need to put additional plans in place. Planning is very critical to your success, and our prayer is that the strategies and tools in this book will help you to plan. If you are not one who plans, or someone who is a strategic thinker as it pertains to your business and creativity, let us try to change your mind now. Here is what the bible has to say about *planning*.

**The plans of the diligent lead surely to abundance, but everyone who is hasty comes only to poverty.**
**Proverbs 21:5**

**Commit your work to the Lord, and your plans will be established.**
**Proverbs 16:3**

**Many are the plans in the mind of a man, but it is the purpose of the Lord that will stand.**
**Proverbs 19:21**

**But he who is noble plans noble things, and on noble things he stands.**
**Isaiah 32:8**

**Prepare your work outside; get everything ready for yourself in the field, and after that build your house.**
**Proverbs 24:27**

**Desire without knowledge is not good, and whoever makes haste with his feet misses his way.**
**Proverbs 19:2**

**Where there is no guidance, a people falls, but in an abundance of counselors there is safety.**
**Proverbs 11:14**

Become a planner! This book will help as there are several spaces and prompts to help you think through the plans of your business, books, and brands. As you develop your plans, take them before the Lord to ensure that He is the architect and has the final say.

## Partnerships (People)

In the glossary, you will find many scriptures on relationships. Relationships will be a key factor to building your business and making others believers of what God wants to create through you. The Lord will speak through you via your relationships with other Godly individuals. He will coach, counsel, and mentor you through spiritual advisors. He will assign people to you in order that He can work through you to be a blessing. (As a member of the family of Christ, through faith, you are also an heir to the Abrahamic Covenant. In Genesis chapter 12, the Lord told Abraham, that He would not only make him a blessing, but all of the people of the earth would be blessed because of Abraham.) **God not only wants to bless you, but He wants to make you a blessing and partner with you to bless other people.** He will take you from one place to another by giving other believers words of wisdom, prophecy, and knowledge about the plans He has for you. God is always speaking, and you can believe that as someone called to impact the culture and the marketplace, God is speaking to you (and through you). You are indeed His partner in bringing the kingdom of heaven to earth. Stay connected!

One way that I (Caressa) have grown in business is through partnering with other kingdom entrepreneurs. I have worked with and have built friendships with many of today's top coaches, ministers, branding gurus, authors, and the list goes on. When I see someone who I want to connect with, or someone who I want to pour into my life, who I want to coach, or who I would like to coach me, I pray for God to provide a connection between us two, and just like the snap of a finger, it happens. Luke 12:32 tells us, *"Don't worry... For it gives your Father great happiness to give you the Kingdom."* Instead of feeling afraid, intimidated, jealous, or competitive about other brilliant men and women of God who are doing their thing in business, I ask God to provide a way for us to collaborate, and then I wait for Him to move or to provide an open door. Remember, it is the Father's pleasure to give you the kingdom!

On several occasions, the Word shows us that God did not create us to be isolated (in fact, that is when the enemy likes to have his way with us). Therefore, pray for divine partnerships, and realize the manifestation of this prayer is God's will for you and your business. Through divine partnerships and kingdom connections, you will have a greater chance to *Make Them Believers!*

## Marketplace Ministry

It's easy to declare a desire to represent God in the marketplace, arts, our families, and politics, but the question is "How do we go about doing this?" Faith without works is DEAD, so while we are certainly spiritual, this guide is practical. The *Make Them Believers* Workbook answers the question "how?" This guide stands strong on its own in preparing entrepreneurs and authors to excel. However, for the greatest impact, join the Make Them Believers Virtual Retreat, our seven-course companion retreat to this workbook. Visit [makethembelievers.co](makethembelievers.co) to get started at any time.

"Ministry" is the act of expressing and spreading the faith with an ultimate goal to make disciples for Jesus Christ. The "marketplace" is the world of trade or economic activity. Notice that in both definitions of ministry and marketplace, there is a global emphasis. We must think globally and expect to make a global impact through our businesses.

**Marketplace ministry** then is the act of ministering to the world through our work in the marketplace, through implementing both biblical and sound business principles.

**The Great Commission**
**Go and make disciples of all the nations, baptizing them in the name of the Father and the Son and the Holy Spirit. Teach these new disciples to obey all the commands I have given you. And be sure of this: I am with you always, even to the end of the age."**
**Matthew 28:19-20**

We are called to
- make disciples of all nations
- represent the Father, Son and Holy Spirit
- teach what Jesus has taught us.
- be confident that Jesus is with us.

There is a major disconnect between the culture and the body of Christ, which prevents ministry from taking place. The gospel of Jesus and Christian principles are counter-cultural. Marketplace ministers have a unique opportunity to end the disconnect and build bridges by engaging culture from various points in business. The problem in making believers is that people will only believe if our lifestyles and businesses demonstrate that we do things differently, that we've been touched by God, His presence in our businesses has made a difference, and that we actually believe in Him and ourselves. We must be SURE that Jesus is with us and, as a result of this revelation, operate with great confidence.

Long gone are the days of following the culture. We must know and engage the culture, but follow Jesus and allow Him to download creative ideas for us to take the gospel to the culture, through the ministries of our businesses.

## The 7-Mountain Mandate

In 1975, Loren Cunningham, the founder of Youth With a Mission (YWAM) was praying about how to turn the world around for Jesus and saw seven areas. At the same time, other international leaders and missionaries received that same revelation from the Lord. This mandate still exists today. Believers around the world are experiencing a deep calling to devote their businesses to the Lord's work in order to demonstrate the heart and mind of Christ, even in business. In his book *Invading Babylon,* Dr. Lance Wallnau, an international author, speaker, business and political strategist, documents Cunningham's encounter and goes on to explain the seven mountains, and our mandate as believers to occupy them.

Wallnau describes only four possible ways to go about accomplishing this mission. Take a look below:

1. The Church preaches the Gospel, but is separated from culture:
Church + Gospel – Culture = Fundamentalism

2. The Church is gathering for social causes, but not preaching the Gospel:
Church – Gospel + Culture = Liberalism

3. The Gospel is being preached and the culture embraced, but not by the Church:
Gospel + Culture – Church = Parachurch

4. All three are lined up:
Church + Gospel + Culture = Kingdom

(Source: Wallnau, Lance; Johnson, Bill (2013-07-16). Invading Babylon: The 7 Mountain Mandate (p. 56). Destiny Image, Inc.. Kindle Edition.)

With the church (as in body of Christ), the gospel, and the culture aligned we are positioned to bring the kingdom of God to each of those mountains, and with Holy Spirit guiding us, we can excel and become influencers in those areas.

The Make Them Believers Virtual Retreat and this companion workbook infuses the principles of the gospel with practical resources and strategies to engage the business culture.

This workbook (retreat) will help you
- Develop a mindset to monetize your passion
- Identify your target audience
- Develop your brand messaging
- Write compelling non-fiction books quickly
- Push past writer's block
- Understand the steps to publish your book
- Learn how to make believers from followers
- Pitch yourself to media and influencers

We recommend spending three to five days on this workbook with a spiritual retreat mindset. Pray through your work in this book. If you would like the video courses that match this workbook, visit [www.makethembelievers.co](www.makethembelievers.co) and register for the Virtual Retreat. If you have questions at any time during your work through these concepts, contact us at [info@makethembelievers.co](info@makethembelievers.co).

**Get ready to expand your brand strategy to make more believers for what God has called you to do!**

# CHAPTER 1
# MINDSET TO MONETIZE

Do you have the mindset to monetize the vision and dreams that God has placed in your heart? This chapter will serve as your spiritual and mental check-up to **confront, cleanse,** and/or **create** a plan to strengthen your emotions and thinking as you prepare to *Make Them Believers*.

**The 15 behaviors and feelings that hinder growth:**

1. Putting yourself last
2. Controlling others
3. Perfectionism
4. Playing small
5. Assuming the worst
6. Doubting your intuition aka Holy Spirit
7. Addiction
8. Procrastination
9. Toxic relationships
10. Needing the approval of others
11. Fear (Rejection + Success)
12. People Pleasing
13. Anxiety
14. Unresolved Grief
15. Betrayal

**In this training you will learn to:**

1. Identify your *power blocks*
2. Learn how to forgive so you can live up to your potential
3. Learn how to overcome self-sabotage
4. Identify who you are called to
5. Find the power within to be unstoppable
6. Finally live your purpose

**Power Questions:**

1. What are the top 3 behaviors that are holding you back?

2. When was the last time you did this limiting behavior?

3. What has this limiting behavior cost you?

4. Which areas of your life are stuck right now?

5. When was the last time you experienced or did this limiting behavior?

6. Where did you learn this from or when did it begin?

7. Who benefits from this behavior?

8. Is there anyone/anything that you have blamed for not being successful in different areas of your life?

9. Up until now, what was the story you were telling others of what happened to you and areas you were feeling stuck in?

10. Was this power block happening FOR you or to you?

11. Has something you experienced in your life blocked you from reaching your fullest potential?

12. Is there an idea, story, dreams, gifts, talents, or voice that has not been heard because of these blocks?

13. Is your business successful but your personal life (i.e. family, friends, and relationships) not as successful as you would like it to be? Or has this affected your professional success as well?

14. What would happen if you did or didn't stop this behavior?
___

15. Would now be a good time to face your fears and change this behavior?
___

16. What would happen if you did or didn't stop this mindset?
___

17. Would now be a good time to face your fears and change this mindset?
___

18. What is it that you want?
___

19. Is it necessary that you live your purpose and that you go after what is yours?
___

20. Have you been confused on how to fulfill your purpose or where to start?
___

21. Have you taken action towards accomplishing your dreams and purpose but constantly get stuck or blocked?
___

22. Are you finding yourself constantly attracting the same type of negative relationships, situations or people in your life?
___

## 5 Things You Must Know

**Your Purpose Matters**
What if the reason you don't know what you are called to do is that you are called to do something that no one has done before. -Lisa Bevere

**Your Voice Matters**
What will you say or do that may change some else's life?  Caressa J

**Your Destiny Matters**
Lovely one, if you dare to dream you must be brave enough to fight!- Lisa Bevere

**Your Heart Matters**
It's time to heal your heart. -Caressa J

**Your Life Matters**
Say this daily. Victory is mine. Victory today is mine! - Caressa J
There is a miracle with your name on it! -Caressa J

When we experience Doubt + Despair + Discouragement, it can hinder us from reaching our full potential in our lives and in business if we do not take the necessary steps to get clarity on how the experiences affect us. Perhaps you experienced power blocks so that you could:

1. Get into <u>alignment with your assignment.</u>

2. Or, maybe your block happened to get your <u>attention</u> to change your <u>intention</u> on how you live your life.

Perhaps, the block you experienced is a tool; a detour, to bring you closer to where you are suppose to be. Consider this: what if the **doubt, despair,** or **discouragement** that you have experienced were part of a roadmap to get you on the path to **destiny.**

A lot of times, we may feel that we are in the right place or doing the right thing, or you may even feel that you are doing very well, and out of nowhere you're hit with feelings of not having enough. Or perhaps you suddenly lost your passion for the thing that used to light you on fire. Have you experienced feeling like you were not on the right page in your life, business, or even in your relationships? This may mean that it is time for a new chapter. It is time to change your course, because God is getting ready to do exceedingly abundantly above all that you can ask, think, or even imagine. But you have to make a decision to go where He leads.

Perhaps, God wants more for you than you want for yourself. God has given you grace; the ability beyond your ability to do more, give more, see more, and share more with the world. In your life, you have to accept that things aren't going to always go right all of the time. Likewise, that life is tough—not easy— life is full of losses, and, nothing works perfectly. Our bodies don't work perfectly, relationships don't work perfectly, economy, weather—nothing goes as planned or as we would desire for them to one hundred percent of the time. Proverbs 14:13 tells us that our hearts may ache even while we laugh, and at the end of joy, we may experience grief. This tells me that we should expect some bumps along the way, because the world is designed that way.

We're designed to experience loss, but here's the key: we're also designed to grow from it. We will have defeats and disappointments. We have to become okay with God's will, even if His will is to limit our time with some things and people that we may have grown accustomed to. So how do we rise above the unexpected, inevitable losses and disappointments in our lives? How do overcome our power blocks? The answer, although very simple, can be quite complicated. We mourn. We mourn, healthily, unapologetically, and publicly. Matthew 5:4 says, *"Blessed are those who mourn, for they shall be comforted."* There is a blessing in the mourning, which brings me to a second important lesson that I want to share about grief and loss.

The second thing that you need to do is to develop a strategy. The following steps will help you when you're waiting on God to give you a vision for your life and business:

1. Eat healthy. You fast. Fasting helps you to get focused on the task at hand. Fasting positions you to hear from God in order to get the clarity you need to change your mindset so that you can have a mindshift in order to step into a new place.

2. Acknowledge your accomplishments. I am sure that even though you are not where you want to be, you have made major accomplishments in different areas of your life. You may be experiencing marital, professional, family, or health issues, but in those situations you have made positive strides to keep going, growing, and glowing. You know this because you have completed the task of picking up this **WORK**book.

3. Express gratitude. Just as it's beneficial to keep track of what we've done, it's also good to notice what we have. Thank God for what you do have, seek Him and the strategy will come. Refer to Matthew 6:33, *"But seek first the kingdom of God and his righteousness, and all these things will be added to you."*

4. Live your Happy. There is something that you enjoy. There is one thing that makes you smile, laugh, and feel good inside. Do that.

5. Read books. This is your season of growth. This is your season of suddenly. God is getting ready to elevate you to a place of consecutive wins. To be happy is to be blessed, that's why it is important to take the time to acknowledge what He has already done, because God is getting ready to do something bigger than what you've experienced before. Huge doors are opening up for you . Divine favor

and elevation in your area of business. People will know your name; they will wonder where you came from. Get clarity through reading, your knowledge is going to take you to the next level.

6. Move. Dance, exercise, and play. These are all healthy outlets that will give you the mindset to win. They are also great for strategy. Moving gives you the burst of energy that you need to step into the new place.

7. Unplug. Get away from social media and any other distractions. Just relax. Cast your cares on God. This is the time to play, read, express gratitude or even write your own story or journal. Sit still. Pray for ten minutes, listen for ten minutes. Pray for thirty minutes, listen for thirty minutes. Whatever you are comfortable with. This is your time to hear from God and to receive your divine strategy.

8. Create something. Instead of creating a vision board, create a happiness board. Post and paste everything that you are grateful for, this will put you in the mindset of what is to come next. This is genius when it comes to getting in the mindset to strategize.

9. Self-care. Don't forget about you. You may have children, obligations in other places, or you may even be ready to work on your dream master plan. You have to take care of you so that you can feel good and fulfill your destiny. Sometimes the best thing to do when trying to create is to not do anything at all. Managing stress and work-life balance are important. Additionally, self care may include taking a day to visit your therapist or counselor. It is healthy to grow in all areas of our lives; it gives us the ability to continue creating and doing.

**The Six Success Habits**

You Listen
*(There will be times when you have to change your course in business and in life.)*
You recover quickly
You welcome change
You are fearless
You don't ask for permission
You are resourceful

**You are Anointed for Business**

*"In all Labor there is profit."* - Proverbs 14:23

God has given you the power to create wealth.
When there are storms in your life and business, you have to have stamina and endurance.
The word is what sustains you.
The flesh is weak, but the spirit is willing.
The hand of the diligent will rule.
What has stopped you from getting the results you desire?

# Declarations for Entrepreneurs

Today favor will follow me everywhere that I go.

Miracles are happening for me right now.

I am the lender and not the borrower.

I am called to dominate.

There is an unique gift that only I have, and I will use it to bring glory to the Kingdom of God.

I was created for business.

Increase, supernatural favor, and huge doors are opening up for me right now.

I am under an open heaven and everything I ask in Jesus' name will be given to me.

# CHAPTER 2
# BRAND FOUNDATION

*"Because of God's grace to me, I have laid the foundation like an expert builder. Now others are building on it. But whoever is building on this foundation must be very careful. For no one can lay any foundation other than the one we already have—Jesus Christ."*
1 Corinthians 3:10-11

Just as our lives are built on a firm foundation in Jesus, your businesses and brands should be constructed on solid foundations of wisdom and well thought-out plans so that they are sustainable. Use the following chapter to develop a strong brand foundation for every new project or business that you launch. A solid brand foundation will provide you with direction and go-to content for future elements and components of your brand.

## Section 1: Brand Messages and Clarity

### Brand Identity

- BRAND VOICE (adjectives to describe how your brand sounds)
  _____

- BRAND PROMISE (what can you guarantee your clients/customers?)
  _____
  _____

- TARGET DEMOGRAPHIC/DREAM CLIENT (who is your ideal audience - age, race, hobbies, lifestyle choices, pains, problems)
  _____
  _____

### Brand Messages

Get creative. Use this section to brainstorm on various taglines. Then describe why these taglines make sense for your brand, considering your target audience, brand promise and brand voice. Then, think deeper about each tagline and brainstorm on sample program names (books, audio, events, classes, web series, etc.) to support your main taglines. If you are unable to generate enough ideas for the "Program/Topic Examples," your main tagline(s) may not be strong enough.

**TAGLINE OPTION 1:** _____
Why does this tagline make sense for your brand?
_____
_____
_____

**PROGRAM/TOPIC NAME EXAMPLES**
- 
- 
- 

**TAGLINE OPTION 2:** _____
Why does this tagline make sense for your brand?
_____
_____
_____

**PROGRAM/TOPIC NAME EXAMPLES**
- 
- 
- 

**TAGLINE OPTION 3:** _____
Why does this tagline make sense for your brand?
_____
_____
_____

**PROGRAM/TOPIC NAME EXAMPLES**
- 
- 
- 

**TAGLINE OPTION 4:** _____
Why does this tagline make sense for your brand?
_____
_____
_____

**PROGRAM/TOPIC NAME EXAMPLES**
- 
-

**EXAMPLE**

## BRAND PALETTE

# MERAKI COMMUNITY UPLIFT

## BRAND IDENTITY

### ❈ BRAND VOICE

Meraki is the Greek word meaning "to do something with soul, creativity, or love; to put something of yourself into your work." Meraki Community Uplift's brand voice is optimistic, enthusiastic, inspirational, progressive, non-traditional, educating, compassionate, realistic, warm, inviting, inclusive and empowering.

### ❈ BRAND PROMISE

Meraki Community Uplift serves as a catalyst for individuals and communities to empower themselves and each other. Its brand promise is to educate, uplift and empower youth, starting in the Oliver Community of East Baltimore with urban farming/gardening skills. Meraki Community Uplift promises that all of its programs, content and initiatives will be community focused.

### ❈ TARGET DEMOGRAPHIC

The target demographic for Meraki Community Uplift is youth in the Oliver community in Northeast Baltimore. Secondary demographics include families and potential community partners including community stakeholders, businesses and leaders who desire to unite in order to effect change for the children and neighborhood.

## BRAND MESSAGES

### ❈ NOURISHMENT TO RISE

The tagline "Nourishment to Rise" speaks towards Meraki Community Uplift's gardening and planting initiatives. "Nourishment" has a double meaning for food nourishment and also food for the mind/soul. *Nourishment to Rise* is broad enough that it can encompass each of the organization's community-focused initiatives.

**MESSAGE EXAMPLES**
- Gain the *Nourishment to Rise* with Meraki Community Uplift.

**PROGRAM/TOPIC NAME EXAMPLES**
- Nourishment to Rise Community Day or Symposium
- "Nourishment to Rise" may also be the title of a book, newsletter or blog that teaches the community how to sustain themselves through gardening and other unity-focused initiatives.

# BRAND MESSAGES

### ❀ [TOGETHER WE] PLANT, PRODUCE & RISE

The tagline "Plant, Produce & Rise" or "Together We Plant, Produce & Rise" has a double meaning with both "Plant" the verb to place in the ground, or noun as in a living organism and also "Produce" the noun (vegetable) or verb as in make/create. These three words reinforce the brand values and mission of Meraki Community Uplift and its focus on ending the food desert in its community and uniting members of the community to empower each other.

MESSAGE EXAMPLES
- Plant, Produce & Rise with Meraki Community Uplift
- Join Meraki Community Uplift's next Farmer's Market… *Together We Plant, Produce & Rise!*

### ❀ THE CATALYST FOR COMMUNITY TRANSFORMATION

The tagline for "A Catalyst for Community Transformation" brings forth the organization's mission in a succinct way. This tagline may appeal more to corporate partners/sponsors, versus individual members of the community.

# BRAND COLORS

The primary brand color we recommend is green for growth, renewal, survival, health and prosperity. We also recommend a variation of red/orange which symbolizes energy, strength, tenacity and dedication. Orange is also a "youthful" color that speaks to the organization's target demographic.

Green: Growth, Renewal, Survival, Prosperity, Gardening, Strength

Orange: Energy, Youth, Creativity, Determination, Success, Happiness, Stimulation

Blue: Calm, Gentle, Serene

Aqua/Teal: Heart, Harmony, Rejuvenation

Coral: Warmth, Soul

Red: Energy, Desire, Love, Passion, Power (Danger)

*After several revisions, we were able to work with Meraki Community Uplift to finalize their brand foundation, including a tagline and brand colors. See below. For additional support, register for the retreat or Brand Foundation course at makethembelievers.co* **or, email** *info@makethembelievers.co.*

## BRAND PALETTE
# MERAKI COMMUNITY UPLIFT

## BRAND IDENTITY

### BRAND VOICE
Meraki is the Greek word meaning "to do something with soul, creativity, or love; to put something of yourself into your work." Meraki Community Uplift's brand voice is optimistic, enthusiastic, inspirational, progressive, non-traditional, educating, compassionate, realistic, warm, inviting, inclusive and empowering.

### BRAND PROMISE
Meraki Community Uplift serves as a catalyst for individuals and communities to empower themselves and each other. Its brand promise is to educate, uplift and empower youth, starting in the Oliver Community of East Baltimore with urban farming/gardening skills. Meraki Community Uplift promises that all of its programs, content and initiatives will be community focused.

### TARGET DEMOGRAPHIC
The target demographic for Meraki Community Uplift is youth in the Oliver community in Northeast Baltimore. Secondary demographics include families and potential community partners including community stakeholders, businesses and leaders who desire to unite in order to effect change for the children and neighborhood.

## BRAND MESSAGES

### EDUCATE, CULTIVATE, TRANSFORM.****

# BRAND COLORS

The primary brand color we recommend is green for growth, renewal, survival, health and prosperity. We also recommend a variation of red/orange which symbolizes energy, strength, tenacity and dedication. Orange is also a "youthful" color that speaks to the organization's target demographic.

**COLOR PSYCHOLOGY**

Green: Growth, Renewal, Survival, Prosperity, Gardening, Strength
Orange: Energy, Youth, Creativity, Determination, Success, Happiness, Stimulation
Blue: Calm, Gentle, Serene
Aqua/Teal: Heart, Harmony, Rejuvenation
Coral: Warmth, Soul
Red: Energy, Desire, Love, Passion, Power (Danger)

## More about Brand Colors

When you develop your brand colors, consider emotions associated with the various colors and also what they symbolize. The three color wheels that follow will help you.

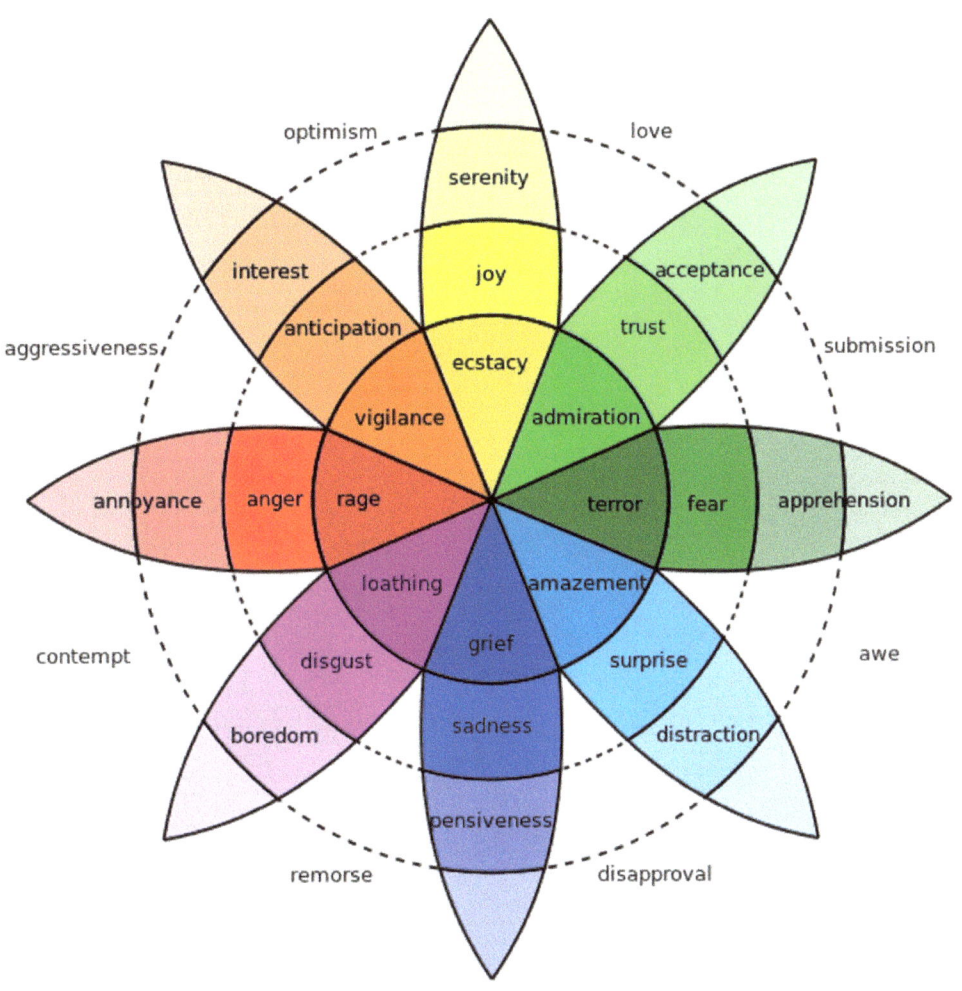

*Robert Plutchik's Wheel of Emotions (Photo credit: Wikipedia via Forbes*

## Color Wheel for Feelings

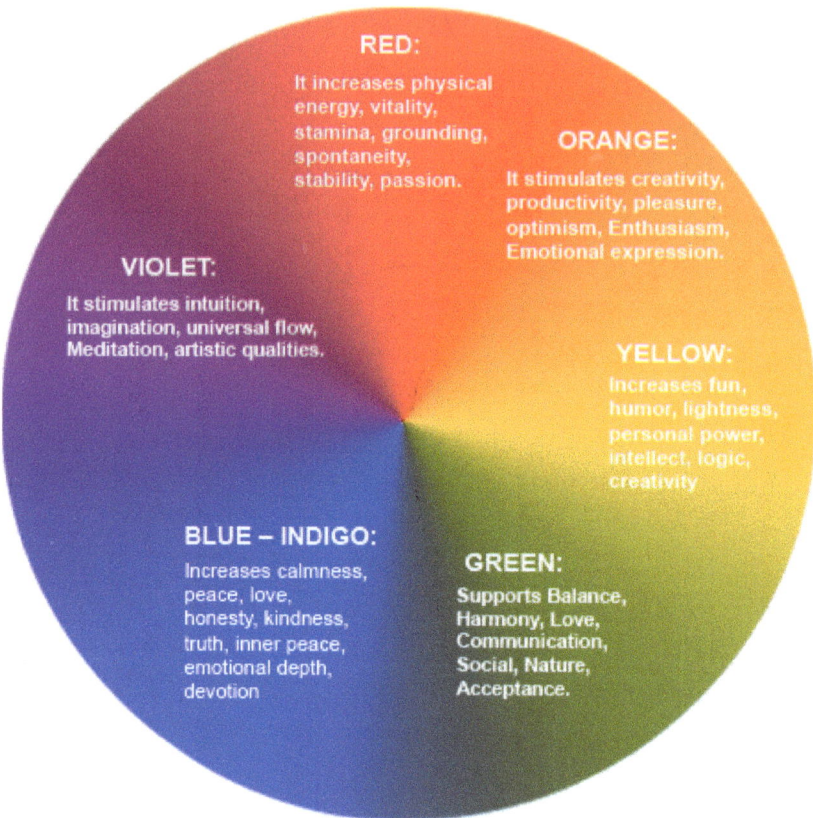

Get Creative!
Think about the emotions you want your brand to evoke. Then, create your own sample palette. You can Google the color name, click on images, and save the color swatches that you like.

Popular brands and their brand colors are explained on the following page.

Via CoSchedule.com

## Section 2: Your Marketing Plan

Your marketing plan will consist of goals, objectives, strategy, tactics, a program(s) and plan. The definitions are below, then there is space for you to work through these elements of your marketing plan.

**Definitions**

Goals are what you hope to achieve. They should be S.M.A.R.T.
**Specific**
**Measurable**
**Achievable**
**Results-Focused**
**Time-Bound**

Objectives are how you will measure success in reaching our goal.

Strategy is an approach that you believe will help you meet your objective.

Tactic is the execution to convert your strategy into action.

Potential Tactics
- Social Media
    - Still video
    - Live video/discussion
    - Curated viral campaign (one announcement, multiple images, multiple people)
    - Word graphics/quotes
    - Photos with compelling stories/little words (minimalist with a link or hashtag)
    - Social media commercials
    - Sponsored posts (see "Ads" below)
- Gorilla Marketing
- Public Relations
- Ads
- Events
- Freebies: Downloads: PDF Tip Sheet, Sample Chapters, Webinar, Audio, Other Video, Product Giveaway, Contests

Program is a collection of related tactics.

Plan is what needs to be done when, given the above. (timeline/schedule)

**Now that you know the terms and definitions, it is time for you to create a plan for your brand. Follow the steps below and refer to the definitions above if necessary.** *You may want to use a pencil here to leave room for edits.*

1. Define your goal

_____

_____

_____

2. Define your objective

_____

_____

_____

3. Brainstorm on a strategy

_____

_____

_____

4. Jot down the tactics

_____

_____

5. What programs can you launch

_____

_____

_____

6. What is the plan including dates

_____

_____

_____

7. List your budget items and amount

_____

_____

_____

***Lastly, ensure that you and your clients have Brand Clarity for your business.***

If you are a service provider, be sure to address and communicate the following four outcomes in your marketing:

1. Functional Outcomes- what does your client or customer achieve as a result of working with you?
2. Financial Outcomes- what can change financially if someone goes through your program? How can you save them time and money?
3. Emotional Outcomes- what is the transformation that your client will receive? What does it look like when they are done working with you?
4. Mental Outcomes- when working with your client, how do you help them gain clarity in a certain area?

## MARKETING MESSAGE CLARITY EXAMPLES

Tagline: Discover how to have a happy everything

Marketing message (or Brand Promise)

Hi My name is (your name _____)
_____

_____

I help (audience/niche + brand promise)
_____

_____

Get more/create more/ lose more (problem you solve)
_____

_____

That allows them to (benefit here)
_____

_____

Examples: My name is _____, and I help business-minded women build six-figure companies while working full-time jobs:
- I help women bounce back to happy and live a life that is fulfilled and courageous
- I help influencers experience transformation and go from tragedy to triumph

**My dream client:**
Needs help with their everyday struggle. Maybe wants to be an entrepreneur but can't move into the next phase or starting a business.
In school or not focused because she's focused on the guy, worth and value, dealing with rejection, offense, or unforgiveness.
Women entrepreneurs: they are successful in business but desire support in their personal lives.

**Program Examples**

**1. Coaching Packages**
The Comeback Power
A 4-week Intensive to Bounce Back To Happy

Private Coaching: $997
Payment Plan: 2 payments $500

4 weeks of coaching
Weekly coaching calls
Email support

Goals:
Quarterly: 30 client a quarter 10 a month
Discovery calls: Clarity calls

**2. Live event**
VIP day with a group of women 1 ½ day $497
4-6 women

**3. Mini Courses**
Topics: Offense, Rejection, fear self sabotage, purpose

**Example: Live your Happy $97- $197 (self- study)**
Module 1: How to find true happiness
Module 2: Living your Happy
Module 3: How to overcome self-sabotage
Module 4: How to practice forgiveness

Modules can be from 10-30 mins

==Think of the outcome you want your customer/client to have and focus the lessons around that.==

Once you record your videos, add them to your Vimeo account or natively upload them to a course content website.

## 4. Freebies
#1  Automated audio
#2 PDF Guide
#3 Free Webinar

**Title:** The ultimate guide to bounce back to happy

**What's included in the guide:**

1. How to….
2. You will learn…
3. You will be able too…

**Webinar**
- Choose Topics that answer the question to a problem or challenge someone maybe facing.

*In the virtual retreat edition of this class, get tips for creating fun branding boards on Pinterest. Visit [makethembelievers.co](makethembelievers.co) to register.*

# CHAPTER 3
# THE AUTHOR'S MASTER CLASS

Like most people, you probably have a story or book idea in your head. Maybe you continuously start and stop, or you haven't begun writing because you don't know where to start. Some of our clients never realize they are authors with a book just waiting to be published until we ask them this question: ==do you constantly find yourself helping others in a specific area?== If so, it's time to write and publish, because you are an expert. **This advice applies to you as well!**

The Author's Masterclass chapter is divided into four easy steps to take you from the beginning to the end of your writing and publishing process. Contact us at info@makethembelievers.co if you need additional support.

## STEP 1: PLAN YOUR BOOK

What's your book goal (why are you writing it)?

_____

What type of book are you writing?

_____

Who is the target audience for your book (be specific)? Example: Women, 18-40, Growing up in urban areas.

_____

Who are the secondary audiences? Example: Younger teens, Husbands of primary audience?

_____

What are they going to get out of it? Write your purpose below. Example: What will the reader leave with? Complete this sentence from your reader's perspective.
**This book was amazing because it ...**

_____

_____


Practice writing a short synopsis (summary for the back of book) below

> **STOP HERE. IT'S TIME TO PLAN YOUR BOOK.**
>
> *What time of day are you most creative? Schedule one hour each day to write for the next 30 days.*

**MY WRITING SCHEDULE**

| Sunday | Monday | Tuesday | Wednesday | Thursday | Friday | Saturday |
|--------|--------|---------|-----------|----------|--------|----------|
|        |        |         |           |          |        |          |

**OUTLINE YOUR BOOK**

An outline will help you plan each chapter, stay focused, and know exactly where you're headed next. If you don't know how to create an outline, no worries, we've got you covered!

**CREATE YOUR OUTLINE**

**Step 1:** On the "a." lines below, list the major points of your book? These can potentially become chapters.
 (Hint: Just do a "brain dump" of topics. It doesn't have to be organized or perfect at this time. Use the a lines to do this.)
**Step 2:** On the "b." lines, summarize what you want to say about this point.
**Step 3:** On the "c." lines, think deeper and ask, "What else does the reader need to know?"
**Step 4:** Under each main point, list the additional research needed to complete the idea.

**Book Outline**

### Chapter 1
a. _____

    b. _____

        c. _____

Additional Research:

### Chapter 2
a. _____

    b. _____

        c. _____

Additional Research

### Chapter 3
a. _____

    b. _____

        c. _____

Additional Research

### Chapter 4
a. _____

    b. _____

        c. _____

Additional Research

## Chapter 5

a._____

b._____

c._____

Additional Research

## Chapter 6

a._____

b._____

c._____

Additional Research

## Chapter 7

a._____

b._____

c._____

Additional Research

## Chapter 8

a._____

b._____

c._____

Additional Research

# SAMPLE BOOK OUTLINE

Book Title: *Cheerleading is a Sport! ... Especially in College*

1. Cheerleaders practice hard
    a. Discuss my college practice schedule (2 a days)
      b. Typical Practice, Cardio, Gymnastics, Dance/cheer
        c. Weightlifting and why not just anybody can do this.
          d. Discuss the importance of weightlifting
    Additional Research: statistics for career success rates for college cheerleaders; cheer testimonials about benefits of being a cheerleader.

2. Cheerleaders compete
    a. Discuss the various competition seasons
      b. Share typical competition weekend
        c. Camaraderie built during competition
          d. We have "March Madness" Season too
    Additional Research: Confirm NCA, MEAC, and other college cheer tournaments. Include total number of college cheerleading competitions.

3. Cheerleaders get college scholarships
    a. How to get a cheerleading scholarship
      b. Level of performance and minimum skills you need
        c. Why schools give cheerleaders scholarships
          What are top cheerleading schools
    Additional Research: Amount of cheerleading scholarships awarded each year.

# STEP 2: WRITE YOUR BOOK

> **HELPFUL TIP:**
>
> *If you're not a writer, no problem. Use a voice recorder or a voice typing app as you talk through your book. If you visit docs.google.com, you can use their "Voice Typing" tool to get your book out of your head.*

## Time to write!

Here's a sample template for nonfiction books. This is simply a recommendation for those of you who are unsure of how to start.
- Quote - begin chapters with a quote, scripture, fact, statement, etc.
- Claim - what is the big idea you are proposing in this chapter?
- Anecdotes - tell a story related to your claim to drive home the point.
- Teaching moment - reiterate what you've taught by stating it plain and simple or in another creative way.

### Steps
1. First write or voice type through your outline (talk into a voice recorder that will type what you say). Go through each point on the outline and do another "brain dump" with each point.
2. Be detailed, be specific, and put all thoughts related to each point under the corresponding bullet point. After you finish writing/talking through your outline, you will have a strong first draft.
3. Next, go into each chapter and conduct your "Additional Research," and add it to your manuscript per chapter.
4. Clean it up. This is when you self edit, add more details, and stories. Make it interesting.
5. After you have a clean draft, you are ready for editing. If you need editing support, contact us at info@makethembelievers.co.

**WRITING PROMPTS TO COMBAT WRITER'S BLOCK**
- **Prompt 1:** Select a chapter or major theme from your book, such as "Forgiveness." Write a personal story about a time when you had to forgive or needed forgiveness for your own behavior. Describe the internal conflict you experienced.
- **Prompt 2:** What hurts most about your story?
- **Prompt 3:** Why are you angry? Write them a letter.
- **Prompt 4:** Write God a letter or journal about your feelings/emotions. As He speaks back to you, write what He's telling you.
- **Prompt 5:** What is the most exciting part of this story?
- **Prompt 6:** Tell your best friend (in writing) the best part of the book.
- **Prompt 7:** Listen to your favorite song; write a line that sticks out to you, and allow your thoughts to flow on paper from there.
- **Prompt 8:** How did you get in this situation? When did it start? Be specific.
- **Prompt 9:** Think about some themes from your journals.

Write from

Hindsight - perception of the nature of an event after it has happened

Foresight - the ability to predict or the action of predicting what will happen or be needed in the future.

Insight - the act or result of apprehending the inner nature of things or of seeing intuitively.

**TIPS TO FILL THE PAGES**
- For non-fiction books, think of a personal story to share with each of your main points and build out from there.
- Use popular culture examples.
- Hypothetical "what-if" situations. (i.e. Imagine this…)
- Dialogue
- Statistics about your topic. Explain/analyze them based on your topic/audience.
- Include scripture and bible stories to support your points.
- Include newspaper headlines or hot-topic issues.

**ELEMENTS OF YOUR BOOK (In order)**
- Title Page
- Copyright Page
- Dedication Page (*optional*)
- Acknowledgements (*optional*)
- Testimonials (*optional*)

- Table of Contents
- Foreword *(optional)*
- Introduction
- Book Content
- About the Author
- Promotion Next/Upcoming Book *(optional)*

## STEP 3: MARKET YOUR BOOK

Your book launch will depend on the time and resources you have (financial and people resources). We've listed several launch models below. Regardless of which one suits your brand best, you want to be sure to implement these best practices "Do's and Don'ts...".

### Do's and Don'ts of Book Marketing for Self-Published Authors

- Do start marketing while you're writing.
- Do market your book for three to six months in advance.
- Do begin building your audience by promoting your list-signup before you begin book pre-sales.
- Do have your book cover designed and your synopsis written early in the process.
- Do begin pre-sales once you have your cover and synopsis.
- Don't pre-sale on Amazon or other online outlines who pay you royalties if your main concern is to make a profit.
- Do build your own platform to sell your book (i.e. personal website) and pre-sale your book there. You keep all of your profits on your own website, whereas third parties will pay you royalties of fifty to seventy percent of your book retail price.
- Don't depend on strictly third party outlets.
- Do pre-sale on Amazon if you are concerned about making a bestseller list and would like to expand your reader audience. Note. you can still make these lists once the book comes out. Sometimes, it's best to add your book to Amazon and other retailers once it has been released (verses in pre-sales) AND once you have exhausted sales from your immediate network.
- Do pitch your book to bloggers, journalists, and book review writers months prior to your release date.
- Do plan a live or online launch event series.
- Think past your book launch event and pre-plan a book tour. There are several ways to do this, which we discuss during our free classes and virtual retreats (makethembelievers.co/classes)

Goals:
1. Sell Books
2. Gain attentions from Influencers and Media
3. Position yourself as a _____
4. Make a difference with your writing.

Other goals??? Refer to the worksheets in section 1.

## PLAN YOUR LAUNCH

### Engage Influencers
Ask popular business, social, media, industry influencers who can connect with your target audience to share the book with their fanbase. Get a quote, picture or video with these individuals to promote on your platforms as well. You need several months to plan for this. We recommend three! This type of book launch is great for people who have great relationships with various influencers.

### Engage Community
What communities would be interested in your book topic? How can you involve them through partnerships, outreach, etc? (Examples: College organizations, fraternities/sororities, co-workers, clients, students, moms, neighbors, military, lodges, cancer community, survivors of similar tragedies, associations).

### Engage your Warm Market
Develop a launch team of people who know and love you. Develop a content calendar and plan of action for what the team will do. Engage with them on a regular basis and reward them for being a part of your team. Create a central communications platform such as a private Facebook group or a Groupme chat group.

### Engage and Build your List
You want to always build your list and continuously engage with subscribers once you've captured their attention. Offer freebies such as sample content to attract new subscribers.

### Engage the Ideal Audience you Don't Know
Social media opens the door to the ideal audience you've never met. Use Facebook, Instagram, and Twitter ads and target people based on their interests and your book demographics. Refer to the DIY… chapter for additional ideas. Depending on your budget, you may also want to advertise on popular blogs or websites.

### Engage the Social Butterflies
Plan your book launch event. Solidify an event venue and date at least three months in advance if possible, and have a public book signing and reading.

### Continue to Build

Launching is a short period of time. Keep pumping life into your book programs with consistent on and offline campaigns, intriguing emails, and creative engagement opportunities.

On the following three pages, begin to plan your book launch, pre-plan a marketing activity that you will implement each day for 60 days. Your steps can start small on day 60 and get bigger as you approach your launch date. Begin marketing and pre-sale while you are still writing.

### Reminders

Do not wait until are are done writing and ready to publish before you begin marketing your book.

**You only need these three items to begin marketing and selling your book:**
1. Book Cover.
2. Book Synopsis.
3. Platform for Book Sales (website, paypal, etc.)

Be sure that you have defined your book goals, etc. Do not skip the previous steps in this chapter.

For more support with this, contact us at [info@makethembelievers.co](mailto:info@makethembelievers.co).

## Promotional Plan - 60-Day Countdown

| Date | Activity |
|---|---|
| Day 60 | |
| | |
| | |
| | |
| | |
| | |
| | |
| | |
| | |
| | |
| | |
| | |
| | |
| | |
| | |
| | |
| | |
| | |
| | |
| | |
| | |

## Promotional Plan - 40-Day Countdown

| Date | Activity |
|---|---|
| Day 40 | |
| | |
| | |
| | |
| | |
| | |
| | |
| | |
| | |
| | |
| | |
| | |
| | |
| | |
| | |
| | |
| | |
| | |
| | |
| | |
| | |

**Promotional Plan - 20-Day Countdown**

| Date | Activity |
|---|---|
| Day 20 | |
| | |
| | |
| | |
| | |
| | |
| | |
| | |
| | |
| | |
| | |
| | |
| | |
| | |
| | |
| | |
| | |
| | |
| | |
| | |

## STEP 4: PUBLISH YOUR BOOK

*Your Steps*
- Book Cover Design
- Book Synopsis Writing
- Editing
- Proofreading
- Typesetting (layout design)
- Proofread again
- ISBN & Barcode  - myidentifiers.com/
- Copyright - copyright.gov
- Publish and Distribute (Print on Demand & Ebook Options)
    - Amazon Kindle (e-book)
    - CreateSpace
    - Barnes & Noble Nook (ebook)
    - iTunes (e-book)
    - Books-a-Million (ebook)
    - Ingram
    - Lulu.com

*Send print copies of your book to the copyright office once you receive print copies.*

Need support? Brown & Duncan Brand's Publish Author Program may be a good fit for you:
http://www.banddbrand.com/authorpackages

# CHAPTER 4
# CUT THROUGH THE NOISE TO BE HEARD

The way to be heard is to know who you are - your unique value, what you offer, and who you are designed to serve. Refer to your work from chapter two and continue building below. If you become stressed out in the process of "trying to be heard," stop and pray, retreat from social media, review Chapter 1, and recommit your business and brand to God. Remember, that these are His plans, and if He called you to it, it will see you through it. God never calls us to something only to leave us hanging. He's got you. Do not be anxious for anything, not even success.

Step 1: Gain Media Attention
- Identify the media outlets that deliver to your target audience.

  *List them here:*


- Write your pitch and/or press release (Refer to Pitch Like a Pro chapter). Press releases should be one page, ideally, but can go into two.


Step 2: Build your Email List and Prospects
1-> Develop an offer "bait" and use Facebook Ads, Instagram Marketing, etc. to drive traffic to your offer.

2-> Your bait should lead to a landing page that you've developed with an email capture and a case study (such as a video/audio about why your offer is so great).

3-> From landing (sales) page, lead visitors to an appointment scheduler.

4-> Meet with prospect (and/or)

5-> Send a series of follow-up emails to sell your offer.

Step 3: Increase your Followers
There are 5 steps to take when you have a goal to increase your social media followers. The answer to this challenge is content and creative storytelling where the potential client sees themselves in the story. People want to connect with you as a human, not an intangible brand.

1. Help people avoid mistakes.
2. Share a powerful testimony.
3. Tell your story.
4. Tell a story showcasing your experience in your industry, topic, and or field.
5. Show people mistakes that are holding them back from reaching the results they desire.
6. Debunk the myths.
7. Remind people why your message is important.

By consistently nurturing your audience, you will keep them engaged and interested in what you have to offer. If you are challenged with identifying who your dream client is and or how to serve your audience take the following five steps.

**Identify:** Determine who you are talking to and what/why they need your business?
**Freebie:** Give something away to validate your idea and give your audience a sneak peek of your product. Remember the freebie should emphasize the what and why, and your paid products should show how to achieve the result with your product.
**Low Cost Offer:** Share a low cost offer that helps your audience fall into your brand. It's a no brainer offer that allows a client to start working with your business. Your low cost offer is meant to educate your audience and start building trust by providing great value and a product that will help your audience.
**Nurture your audience:** Nurturing will be one of the most important steps and you will be able to build in repeat or returning customers. Your clients need to hear from you on a consistent basis and get to know you.
**Offer:** The difference between a hobby and having a successful business is an offer. Offers are important because this is how 1) You increase sales 2) Provide a solution to a problem and 3) even if they don't purchase everything, your audience will know you have products available.

Step 4: Gain Clientele
Problem + Solution = Transformation

As the expert what problem do you solve?

Step 5: Make Them Believers!

Consistency + Content + Customer Appreciation = Brand Loyalty

**How to Build a Brand that Attracts Clients Quickly**
In order to start building your attractive brand quickly, ask yourself the following questions:
1. How do you want to be remembered?
2. How do you want to show up in the world?
3. How do you want people to feel?

**Do you have the confidence you need to take your brand to the next level?**
A lack of confidence can show up in your brand.

**Do you understand who your customers are?**
Gain clarity on who your customers are, the message that you want to send out and how you want to help people.

**Do you give massive value**
You are never giving away too much information (value) the more value you give, the more clients you attract.

*Show up confidently and the right people will be attracted to you.

==*Remember that your free content and social media posts are not your business, they are your bait, meaning marketing tools that direct customers to your paid offers.==

# CHAPTER 5:
# PITCH LIKE A PRO

There are many platforms such as print and digital magazines, newspapers, blogs, radio, television broadcasts, and radio. Once you become an expert in your niche, clarify your message and identify your ideal audience, you will be able to pitch and share your message with the masses.

**Will the media want to cover you?**
- Are you planning a charitable initiative to make a difference in your community?
- What is currently HOT in the media?
- Do you have advice or a solution to a problem that will help someone mentally, emotionally, or financially?
- Have you been successful at something in which you want to show others how to be successful as well?
- Do you have an upcoming event?
- Did you write an amazing book and are ready to go on a book tour?

These are all pitch worthy causes!

What holiday or national event can your current strategy or solution help?
If you are a dating expert, and it is Christmas time, can you give advice on the perfect gift people can give their significant others, if they are not ready to tie the knot yet?
If you are a domestic violence survivor, do you have a story + book or program that will inspire or help others? Or, do you have tips coupled with your story to help others remain safe?

**Develop Your Pitch**
**Problem:** September 11th is coming up in two months, as a grief and loss expert, I (Caressa) can provide tips on how to deal with loss, adversity, breakups, death etc.
**Quick Pitch:** How to cherish memories of loved ones that lost their lives during a national tragedy.

**Problem:** You are a dating expert and Valentine's Day is in two months
What type of media pitches would you send to editors?
**Quick pitch:**
How to make up with your ex before Valentine's Day
5 ways to spark it up with your mate

**Email Pitch Example to Media**

A similar approach can be used for phone pitches/cold calls. Here is an example of eal pitch used for both email and phone pitches.

Hello [NAME], my name is _____ and I am reaching out to you on behalf of Author, Wedding Planning Expert and Towson University Professor ___. She is launching The _____ Tour this month (May 31) in Philadelphia, and I thought this could be an event that would interest your audience. The tour will merge faith and finance principles to help aspiring and new entrepreneurs profit in their purpose. Below is a press release with details about our Philadelphia speakers. Please let me know if you would be able to share this with your audience, and/or if you are interested in speaking with our client.

Thank you so much!
Name
Phone Number

<copy and paste press release below in email.>

---

**Sample Pitch to Secure Bookings**

*Note that more casual email introductions with linked media often works better than a formal press releases.*

Authors of *Make Them Believers!* Teach Business Principles to Ministries
*Secure Talent for your Upcoming Events*

(Washington, DC) – *Make Them Believers Academy has released its* strategy workbook to help believers in business excel in the marketplace. In this book, Authors Natasha T. Brown and Caressa Jennings share successful strategies that have helped them transform many of today's church leaders into inspirational authors and marketplace ministers. Through intimate live and virtual workshops and conferences, the concepts in *Make Them Believers* are empowering ministers of the Gospel to occupy the seven mountains of society.

Below are a list of topics that *Make Them Believers* authors teach. To secure a conference, workshop, or retreat for your ministry, contact info@makethembelievers.co.

Topics:
-Ministry in the Marketplace
-Mindset to Monetize
-Digital Evangelism
-Write and Publish Bestselling Books
-Package and Pitch Powerful Brand Messages .

To order copies of the book, visit makethembelievers.co
{Author Bios}

# Sample Press Release (Initiative)

For Immediate Release
[Date]
Contact:

## The EZ Street Show Debuts On Television in May
*National Radio Personality Creates Washington, DC Focused Magazine Show*

(Washington, DC) — *The EZ Street Show People, Places, Things DC* will make its television debut on the District of Columbia Network on May XX, as a weekly entertainment and lifestyle show spotlighting issues affecting the Nation's Capital. The EZ Street Show launched in 1995 on 93.9 WKYS FM and has since become synonymous with Washington, DC culture-community-music, and entertainment. With the show's expansion to television, Executive Producer EZ Street will provide a voice to important people and issues that are often excluded from mainstream news, while also keeping the lighthearted and fun feel *The EZ Street Show* is known for.

"This television show will give a voice to people who don't have a voice, in a visual and captivating way. My goal is to make The EZ Street Show a reflection of Washington, DC, by bringing stories to life that are not being told," said EZ Street. "We're going to provide content that you can't find anywhere else, and it's going to be fun."

The inaugural broadcast of *The EZ Street Show* on DCN will take viewers into "A Day In The Life of Black Transgender DC." *The EZ Street Show* also captured behind-the-scenes details of the DC Library's Go-Go Preservation project. The show will be a half-hour, with three segments in every episode that range from documentary-type feature stories, celebrity interviews and event features.

Watch *The EZ Street Show* in DC on [LIST CHANNELS & DAYS OF THE WEEK] at [LIST TIMES OF BROADCASTS]. Each show will also be available on YouTube.com/EZStreetShow following the original broadcasts.

To request coverage by *The EZ Street Show* or to request an interview with EZ Street, contact XXXX.

### About EZ Street
EZ Street, a noted national radio host and community activist, is the midday personality on 93.9 WKYS from 10am to 3pm. He is also the host of Trending with EZ on sister station WOL 1450 AM. In addition to his radio career, EZ Street is a devoted father, marine corp veteran, film director and deacon at Union Temple AME Church in Washington, DC.

###

**Write Your Sample Media Pitch Below!**

# CHAPTER 6
# D.I.Y. OR PAY-TO-PLAY?

***Purpose + Power Resources + Tech Tools***

In this final chapter, you will learn various business building tools. The first section covers "D.I.Y." resources that you can use to create elements of your brand for yourself. The second section covers a list of recommended service providers to consider for coaching, design, etc. Finally, there's a "How to" section.

We share specifics on how and when to use these tools in the Virtual Retreat. Signup at [makethembelievers.co](makethembelievers.co), this class is called D.I.Y. or Pay-to-Play.

## Tools to Do It Yourself

**Stock Photos**
Unsplash
Stocksy
Scstockshop.com
Bigstockphoto.com
stock.adobe.com/stock_photo (free month's trial)
shutterstock.com/
pexels.com (free)

**Web Payment Options**
Moonclerk.com
Samcart.com
Paypal.com
Woocommerce
Stripe.com

**Email Marketing/Member Sites**
Mailchimp.com
Aweber.com
Simplero.com
Privy.com
ConstantContact.com

Activecampaign.com

**Course Platforms**
Teachable.com
Thinkific.com
NewKajabi.com
Wishlistmember.com

**Course Editing**
Screenflow (MAC)
Camtasia (PC User)

**Webinar Platforms**
Webinarjam.com
Zoom.us
YouTube Live/Google Hangouts

**Self-publishing**
Createspace.com
Ingram.com
BookBaby.com
LuLu.com

**Designing Graphics**
PicMonkey
Canva
Adobe Spark
Photoshop
Acorn (program similar to Photoshop, but less expensive)

**Fonts/Typeface (for Logos, etc)**
DaFont.com
Fonts.com
fonts.google.com

**Record + Edit your course**
Screenflow (Mac Users)
Camtasia (PC Users)

**Website Platforms**
Squarespace.com
Wix.com
Webs.com
Wordpress.com

**Sales Pages**
Leadpages — They have a lot of customizable templates to choose from. We recommend LeadPages for creating landing/squeeze pages (i.e. the page you send people to sign up for something — a webinar, freebie gift, more information, etc).

OptimizePress — This theme/plugin allows you to easily create sales pages and membership sites that are highly customizable.

ClickFunnels — Create an automated sales funnel for your online business.

Privy.com — They have free and paid options for email automation, landing pages, and website email captures.

**Podcast**
Record your podcast on your voice recorder on phone and upload to Soundcloud.com for FREE and link it after uploading to Itunes and Google Music Play
You can also use FreeConferencePro.com to record calls and download the MP3s. Zoom.us is also good to record video and audio at the same time, to be used as Podcasts, web videos, etc.

**To Host PDF content**
Amazon S3 — Host your course content here
DropBox
Google Drive & Google Docs
Directly from Websites such as Wordpress or Squarespace

**To Host videos:**
In order to make sure that your videos aren't accessible to non customers you can host them on YouTube.com (for free) and make them private so you can embed them onto your membership site.

Vimeo Pro — At $59.95/year, it's an affordable option if you have multiple online courses or run your online course multiple times a year.

Wistia — $25/month, This has more analytics and information than Vimeo Pro. Very easy to embed and used by a lot of the pros.

Wishlist Member — $299.00 one time fee and you build your own custom website
The following platforms were built for the sole purpose of making it easy for you to run your online course.

Memberful
Kajabi
Teachable

**Creating your EBook**
Pages (for Mac users)
Word (for PC users)
Canva — Choose "Use custom dimensions" on the homepage and enter the document size (8.5" x 11"). And then use the drag and drop editing features to design your eBook cover.
Directly into Kindle (kdp.amazon.com) or iBooks

*Note: Amazon Kindle prefers text files over PDFs. PDF documents uploaded as e-books usually come out distorted in certain places.*

**To create a 3D mockup of your eBook cover, you can use Adazing and Boxshot.**

# Pay-to-Play

**Book Publishing**
BandDBrand.com/schedule
*(Schedule a free Book Discovery Session)*

**Branding/Brand Coaching**
BandDbrand.com
Creativelyflawless.com
TressaAzarelVIPClub.com

**Coaching Platforms**
Jigsawbox.com
Expertise.tv

**Clarity Coaching for Coaches & Celebpreneurs**
CaressaJ.com

**Graphic Design**
Banddbrand.com
Crftd.online
Caseyrenae.com

**Marketing & Business Schools**
Makethembelievers.co
Tiphanimontgomery.com

**Photography**
Roycoxphotography.com
Patrickmossphotography.com
Rheawhitneyphotography.com
Ashleighbingphotography.com

**Public Relations**
Email us for recommendations at info@makethembelievers.co

**Website Content +Copy Editor +Book Writing**
BandDbrand.com
Wordsbystef.com

Iamdrnes.com
Ebeetbee.com

**Business must haves**
LLC/DBA/Sole Proprietorship
LOGO
Business Bank Account
Business Paypal
PO Box
Domain and Website
Active Social Media Accounts
Marketing Materials (i.e. Business Card, media kit, flyers)

**Business Cards**
Moo.com
Peppermint Print

**Trademark/Copyright**
Copyright.gov
Trademarkia.com

**Business & Legal Consultation**
www.savvyesq.com
www.nakiagray.com
Privacy Policy, Terms + Conditions
Trademark Filing
Legal Toolkit
Contracts

**Book Distributors**
http://www.ibpa-online.org/page/distributors

**External Microphones**
Blue Yeti
Blue Snowball

**DISCOVERY CALL CHECKLIST** (Goals are to learn is this a dream client + are we a good fit + can they afford services)

**SOCIAL MEDIA MARKETING CHECKLIST**
- A hot OFFER
- Freebie (Lead Magnet)
- Landing Page
- A sales process
- FB ad budget or Social Media Post

**Ways to grow your audience**
- Public Speaking
- Vending at events
- Podcast
- Guest Blogging
- Media Features
- FB Ads
- Write a book (Solve a problem)
- Partnerships
- Referrals
- Live Streaming (FB and Periscope)
- Brand Ambassador Program

***Last but not least, be sure that your***

- Social media name is consistent on all platforms
- Pictures and content on social media are consistent with website
- Tagline or call-to-action (CTA) are in headlines
- Social media template is consistent (Create a template on canva for free using your brand colors and font to give free content on social media)
- Marketing includes live video such as Periscope and Facebook Live (Video Marketing is the #1 type of marketing to use)
- Social media posts are daily with business related content and/or storytelling
- Brand offers free content… The more free content you provide, the more valuable you appear to your customer
- ==Website content focuses on client transformation. What solution do you solve for your customer's problem?==

## You are ready to *Make Them Believers!*

# Topical Scripture Glossary for Entrepreneurs

# AFFIRMATION

But thank God! He has made us his captives and continues to lead us along in Christ's triumphal procession. Now he uses us to spread the knowledge of Christ everywhere, like a sweet perfume.
**2 Corinthians 2:14**

But you are a chosen race, a royal priesthood, a holy nation, a people for his own possession, that you may proclaim the excellencies of him who called you out of darkness into his marvelous light.
**1 Peter 2:9**

Your word is a lamp to my feet and a light to my path.
**Psalm 119:105**

And my God will supply every need of yours according to his riches in glory in Christ Jesus.
**Philippians 4:19**

I can do all things through him who strengthens me.
**Philippians 4:13**

…You are from God and have overcome them, for he who is in you is greater than he who is in the world.
**1 John 4:4**

In him we live and move and have our being…
**Acts 14:28**

But seek first the kingdom of God and his righteousness, and all these things will be added to you.
**Matthew 6:33**

Now all glory to God, who is able, through his mighty power at work within us, to accomplish infinitely more than we might ask or think.
**Ephesians 3:20**

The Lord will perfect *that which* concerns me…
**Psalm 138:8**

# CONFIDENCE

Let us then with confidence draw near to the throne of grace, that we may receive mercy and find grace to help in time of need.
**Hebrews 4:16**

Therefore, if anyone is in Christ, he is a new creation. The old has passed away; behold, the new has come.
**2 Corinthians 5:17**

Because of Christ and our faith in him, we can now come boldly and confidently into God's presence.
**Ephesians 3:12**

I can do all things through Christ who strengthens me.
**Philippians 4:13**

For you formed my inward parts; you knitted me together in my mother's womb. I praise you, for I am fearfully and wonderfully made. Wonderful are your works; my soul knows it very well.
**Psalm 139:13-14**

In all your ways acknowledge him, and he will make straight your paths.
**Proverbs 3:6**

But seek first the kingdom of God and his righteousness, and all these things will be added to you.
**Matthew 6:33**

Therefore do not be anxious about tomorrow, for tomorrow will be anxious for itself. Sufficient for the day is its own trouble.
**Matthew 6:34**

And I am sure of this, that he who began a good work in you will bring it to completion at the day of Jesus Christ.
**Philippians 1:6**

# FEAR

For God gave us a spirit not of fear but of power and love and self-control.
**2 Timothy 1:7**

Give all your worries and cares to God, for he cares about you.
**1 Peter 5:7**

Fear not, for I am with you; be not dismayed, for I am your God; I will strengthen you, I will help you, I will uphold you with my righteous right hand.
**Isaiah 41:10**

There is no fear in love, but perfect love casts out fear. For fear has to do with punishment, and whoever fears has not been perfected in love.
**1 John 4:18**

I sought the Lord, and he answered me and delivered me from all my fears.
**Psalm 34:4**

The fear of man lays a snare, but whoever trusts in the Lord is safe.
**Proverbs 29:25**

Do not be anxious about anything, but in everything by prayer and supplication with thanksgiving let your requests be made known to God.
**Philippians 4:6**

When I am afraid, I put my trust in you. In God, whose word I praise, in God I trust; I shall not be afraid. What can flesh do to me?
**Psalm 56:3-4**

Have I not commanded you? Be strong and courageous. Do not be frightened, and do not be dismayed, for the Lord your God is with you wherever you go."
**Joshua 1:9**

For the Lord will be your confidence and will keep your foot from being caught.
**Proverbs 3:26**

# PERSEVERANCE

For nothing is impossible with God.
**Luke 1:37**

And let us not be weary in well doing: for in due season we shall reap, if we faint not.
**Galatians 6:9**

Blessed is the man who remains steadfast under trial, for when he has stood the test he will receive the crown of life, which God has promised to those who love him.
**James 1:12**

Count it all joy, my brothers, when you meet trials of various kinds, for you know that the testing of your faith produces steadfastness. And let steadfastness have its full effect, that you may be perfect and complete, lacking in nothing.
**James 1:2-4**

For you have need of endurance, so that when you have done the will of God you may receive what is promised.
**Hebrews 10:36**

And I am sure of this, that he who began a good work in you will bring it to completion at the day of Jesus Christ.
**Philippians 1:6**

Rejoice in hope, be patient in tribulation, be constant in prayer.
**Romans 12:12**

Do you not know that in a race all the runners run, but only one receives the prize? So run that you may obtain it.
**1 Corinthians 9:24**

Yet the righteous holds to his way, and he who has clean hands grows stronger and stronger.
**Job 17:19**

Therefore, my beloved brothers, be steadfast, immovable, always abounding in the work of the Lord, knowing that in the Lord your labor is not in vain.
**1 Corinthians 15:58**

# PURPOSE

For I know the plans I have for you, declares the Lord, plans for welfare and not for evil, to give you a future and a hope.
**Jeremiah 29:11**

And we know that for those who love God all things work together for good, for those who are called according to his purpose.
**Romans 8:28**

You did not choose me, but I chose you and appointed you that you should go and bear fruit and that your fruit should abide, so that whatever you ask the Father in my name, he may give it to you.
**John 15:16**

In him we have obtained an inheritance, having been predestined according to the purpose of him who works all things according to the counsel of his will...
**Ephesians 1:11**

The Lord of hosts has sworn: "As I have planned, so shall it be, and as I have purposed, so shall it stand..."
**Isaiah 14:24**

"Before I formed you in the womb I knew you, and before you were born I consecrated you; I appointed you a prophet to the nations."
**Jeremiah 1:5**

For we are his workmanship, created in Christ Jesus for good works, which God prepared beforehand, that we should walk in them.
**Ephesians 2:10**

And I am sure of this, that he who began a good work in you will bring it to completion at the day of Jesus Christ.
**Philippians 1:6**

Commit your work to the Lord, and your plans will be established.
**Proverbs 16:3**

# RELATIONSHIPS

A soft answer turns away wrath, but a harsh word stirs up anger.
**Proverbs 15:1**

There is no fear in love, but perfect love casts out fear. For fear has to do with punishment, and whoever fears has not been perfected in love.
**1 John 4:18**

Then the Lord God said, "It is not good that the man should be alone; I will make him a helper fit for him."
**Genesis 2:18**

Therefore encourage one another and build one another up, just as you are doing.
**1 Thessalonians 5:11**

Above all, keep loving one another earnestly, since love covers a multitude of sins.
**1 Peter 4:8**

This God—his way is perfect; the word of the Lord proves true; he is a shield for all those who take refuge in him.
**2 Samuel 22:31**

With all humility and gentleness, with patience, bearing with one another in love, eager to maintain the unity of the Spirit in the bond of peace.
**Ephesians 4:2-3**

A friend loves at all times, and a brother is born for adversity.
**Proverbs 17:17**

Do not be deceived: "Bad company ruins good morals."
**1 Corinthians 15:33**

This is how I want you to conduct yourself in these matters. If you enter your place of worship and, about to make an offering, you suddenly remember a grudge a friend has against you, abandon your offering, leave immediately, go to this friend and make things right. Then and only then, come back and work things out with God.
**Matthew 5:23-24 MSG**

# STABILITY & STRENGTH

He gives power to the weak and strength to the powerless.
**Isaiah 40:29**

Not that we are sufficient of ourselves to think of anything as *being* from ourselves, but our sufficiency *is* from God...
**2 Corinthians 3:5**

"Blessed is the man who trusts in the Lord, whose trust is the Lord. He is like a tree planted by water, that sends out its roots by the stream, and does not fear when heat comes, for its leaves remain green, and is not anxious in the year of drought, for it does not cease to bear fruit."
**Jeremiah 17:7-8**

My soul, wait silently for God alone, For my expectation *is* from Him. He only *is* my rock and my salvation; *He is* my defense; I shall not be moved. In God *is* my salvation and my glory; The rock of my strength, *And* my refuge, *is* in God.
**Psalm 62:5-7**

Cast your burden on the Lord, and he will sustain you; he will never permit the righteous to be moved.
**Psalm 55:22**

You will seek me and find me, when you seek me with all your heart.
**Jeremiah 29:13**

He who dwells in the secret place of the Most High. Shall abide under the shadow of the Almighty. I will say of the Lord, *"He is* my refuge and my fortress; My God, in Him I will trust." ... Because you have made the Lord, *who is* my refuge, *Even* the Most High, your dwelling place, No evil shall befall you, Nor shall any plague come near your dwelling; For He shall give His angels charge over you, To keep you in all your ways.
**Psalm 91:1-2, 9-11**

But now the Lord my God has given me rest on every side. There is neither adversary nor misfortune.
**1 Kings 5:4**

# SUCCESS

Then God said, "Let Us make man in Our image, according to Our likeness; let them have dominion over the fish of the sea, over the birds of the air, and over the cattle, over all the earth and over every creeping thing that creeps on the earth." So God created man in His *own* image; in the image of God He created him; male and female He created them. Then God blessed them, and God said to them, "Be fruitful and multiply; fill the earth and subdue it; have dominion over the fish of the sea, over the birds of the air, and over every living thing that moves on the earth."
**Genesis 1:26-28**

If you abide in me, and my words abide in you, ask whatever you wish, and it will be done for you.
**John 15:7**

This Book of the Law shall not depart from your mouth, but you shall meditate in it day and night, that you may observe to do according to all that is written in it. For then you will make your way prosperous, and then you will have good success.
**Joshua 1:8**

The Lord shall preserve your going out and your coming in
From this time forth, and even forevermore.
**Psalm 121:8**

Behold, I will bring to it health and healing, and I will heal them and reveal to them abundance of prosperity and security.
**Jeremiah 33:6**

All Scripture is breathed out by God and profitable for teaching, for reproof, for correction, and for training in righteousness, that the man of God may be competent, equipped for every good work.
**2 Timothy 3:16-17**

But the Helper, the Holy Spirit, whom the Father will send in my name, he will teach you all things and bring to your remembrance all that I have said to you.
**John 14:26**

# WEALTH

For bodily exercise profits a little, but godliness is profitable for all things, having promise of the life that now is and of that which is to come.
**1 Timothy 4:8**

A good *man* leaves an inheritance to his children's children,
But the wealth of the sinner is stored up for the righteous.
**Proverbs 13:22**

The rich rules over the poor, and the borrower is the slave of the lender.
**Proverbs 22:7**

For which of you, desiring to build a tower, does not first sit down and count the cost, whether he has enough to complete it?
**Luke 14:28**

Blessed is the man who fears the Lord, Who delights greatly in His commandments. His descendants will be mighty on earth; The generation of the upright will be blessed. Wealth and riches will be in his house, And his righteousness endures forever.
**Psalm 112:1-3**

He who loves money will not be satisfied with money, nor he who loves wealth with his income; this also is vanity.
**Ecclesiastes 5:10**

The Lord makes poor and makes rich; he brings low and he exalts.
**1 Samuel 2:7**

In all things I have shown you that by working hard in this way we must help the weak and remember the words of the Lord Jesus, how he himself said, 'It is more blessed to give than to receive.'"
**Acts 20:35**

In all toil there is profit, but mere talk tends only to poverty.
**Proverbs 14:23**

# WISDOM

The fear of the Lord is the beginning of knowledge; fools despise wisdom and instruction.
**Proverbs 1:7**

If any of you lacks wisdom, let him ask God, who gives generously to all without reproach, and it will be given him. But let him ask in faith, with no doubting, for the one who doubts is like a wave of the sea that is driven and tossed by the wind.
**James 1:5-6**

Call to me and I will answer you, and will tell you great and hidden things that you have not known.
**Jeremiah 33:3**

But the wisdom from above is first pure, then peaceable, gentle, open to reason, full of mercy and good fruits, impartial and sincere.
**James 3:17**

Blessed is the one who finds wisdom, and the one who gets understanding, for the gain from her is better than gain from silver and her profit better than gold. She is more precious than jewels, and nothing you desire can compare with her. Long life is in her right hand; in her left hand are riches and honor. Her ways are ways of pleasantness, and all her paths are peace. She is a tree of life to those who lay hold of her; those who hold her fast are called blessed.
**Proverbs 3:13-18**

An intelligent heart acquires knowledge, and the ear of the wise seeks knowledge.
**Proverbs 18:15**

Trust in the Lord with all your heart, and do not lean on your own understanding.
**Proverbs 3:5**

See to it that no one takes you captive by philosophy and empty deceit, according to human tradition, according to the elemental spirits of the world, and not according to Christ.
**Colossians 2:8**

Wisdom *is* the principal thing; *Therefore* get wisdom. And in all your getting, get understanding.
**Proverbs 4:7**

By wisdom a house is built, and by understanding it is established; by knowledge the rooms are filled with all precious and pleasant riches.
**Proverb 24:3-4**

## ABOUT THE AUTHORS

Natasha T. Brown is the *Founder/President of* **10 Blessings Inspiration, Inc.** *and Managing Partner of* **B&D Brand**. *She is a* **brand strategist, book coach, bestselling author and ghostwriter**. As a passionate evangelist and domestic violence advocate, Natasha loves to help others thrive in their God-given purpose spiritually, emotionally and professionally and help survivors of tragedy create strategies for books, brands, missions, and ministries..

After earning bachelor's and master's degrees from Morgan State University (Communications) and Towson University (Professional Writing: Teaching College Writing), Natasha served as a journalist, corporate marketer, development communications associate, and an adjunct writing professor before starting her first communications business in 2009, where she helped over 200 brands share their stories with the world.

Today, she uses her professional and spiritual gifts of writing, strategy, teaching, marketing, evangelism, and coaching to empower others. Natasha is also pursuing a Master's of Divinity Degree in Marketplace Ministry.

Caressa J. is a **Personal Coach and Mentor** to women *visionaries, influencers and celebpreneurs*. Caressa is the owner of **Caressa J. International**, and **Caressa J. Consulting**. An established expert on happiness, healing and heartbreak, her insight has graced the pages of numerous nationally renowned publications and digital media platforms.

Through her signature courses and online platform, she teaches current and aspiring entrepreneurs and business owners on how to get clear about fears, the past, hang ups, and beliefs that are keeping them stuck in their life, so that they can make maximum impact in their business.

Caressa J. is known for her authenticity and straight-from-the-hip approach. A compassionate speaker, she is shifting the modern woman's perspective on life, teaching her how to be genuinely happy, fulfilled and living her purpose. Caressa connects deeply with audiences nationwide, leading women through an intimate, explorative experience from every stage.

Caressa received her Bachelor's degree in Social Work and a Master's of Arts in Human Services: Marriage and Family Therapy. Caressa is a Certified Professional Life Coach and Grief Recovery Specialist.

Was this resource helpful? If so, please share it with your network who can benefit.

Visit MakeThemBelievers.co for more resources, to enroll in upcoming courses, or to schedule consulting sessions with Caressa and Natasha.

Ask us about our special bulk order rate and book us to facilitate a retreat or workshop.
Thank you for your support!

www.ingramcontent.com/pod-product-compliance
Lightning Source LLC
Chambersburg PA
CBHW061144010526
44118CB00026B/2869